TEST 1

閱讀：是非題

請仔細閱讀，看看句子和圖片的內容是不是一樣呢？如果相同，請在答案卡上塗黑 Y；如果不同，請塗黑 N。

1. The girl is washing her hair.
2. The man is watching TV.

正確答案：1. N 2. N

1. There is a radio on the desk.
2. A boy is lying in bed.

3. Each family is sitting at a different table.

4. Two of the men are wearing hats.

	Mon.	**Tue.**	**Wed.**	**Thu.**	**Fri.**	**Sat.**
13:30 | 14:30	clarinet	violin		clarinet	violin	clarinet
15:00 | 16:30	violin	clarinet	piano	violin		violin
18:30 | 20:00	piano		piano	guitar	clarinet	guitar

5. Andy takes piano lessons on Tuesday.

6. Andy takes guitar lessons on Saturday.

7. Ann is eight years old today.

8. There are eight candles on the cake.

9. It's 3:15.

10. The boy is playing a video game.

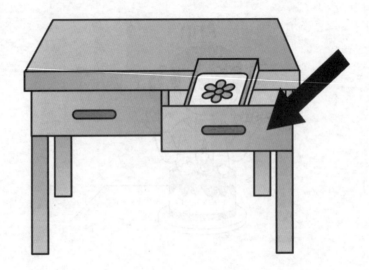

11. The drawer is open.

12. There is a book on the desk.

13. This is a cheeseburger.

14. One slice of pizza is missing.

	work in the garden	go to the concert	listen to music	play sports
Sophia	usually	usually	always	never
Amy	always	often	sometimes	usually
Ben	never	usually	sometimes	often
Harry	sometimes	never	usually	always

※ ● always ◑ usually ◐ often ◔ sometimes ○ never

15. Harry always plays sports.

16. Ben never works in the garden.

17. Two girls are playing with a ball on the beach.

18. Two boys are building castles in the sands.

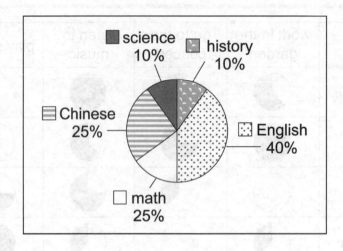

19. English is the least popular subject.

20. Chinese is the most popular subject.

閱讀：選擇題

作答說明：閱讀後，每題請根據文章內容選出一個最適合的答案，在答案卡上作答。

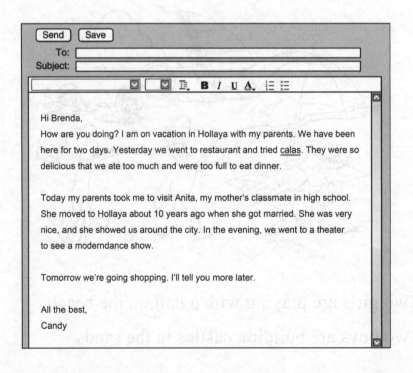

Hi Brenda,

How are you doing? I am on vacation in Hollaya with my parents. We have been here for two days. Yesterday we went to restaurant and tried <u>calas</u>. They were so delicious that we ate too much and were too full to eat dinner.

Today my parents took me to visit Anita, my mother's classmate in high school. She moved to Hollaya about 10 years ago when she got married. She was very nice, and she showed us around the city. In the evening, we went to a theater to see a moderndance show.

Tomorrow we're going shopping. I'll tell you more later.

All the best,
Candy

Where is Candy now?

A. At school.

B. At work.

C. On vacation.

正確答案：C

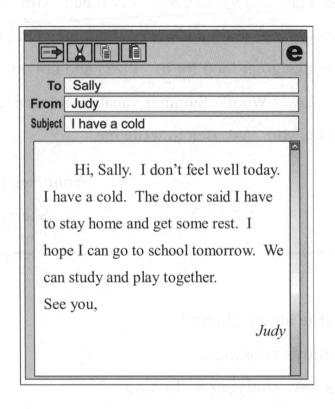

21. What is wrong with Judy?

    A. She broke her arm.

    B. She has a cold.

    C. She didn't finish her homework.

Dear Mom & Dad,

How are you? I'm fine here in Taiwan. All my classmates are nice to me, and my teachers are, too. My PE teacher, Mr. Chen, is really kind to me, and he is also from the US. He is a tall handsome man, and we like him very much. Grace and her family are really nice, so do not worry about me. On Sundays, Grace's dad cooks great food for us. Pizza and hot dogs are my favorite. How's Woof? Summer vacation is coming. I can't wait to see you. Ask Ben to write me.

Your daughter,
Sherry

22. What is true about Sherry?

A. She enjoys cooking.

B. She is now studying in Taiwan.

C. She will spend her summer vacation in Taiwan.

Secret Number

A long time ago, before people could write, they found ways to tell the news. They built a fire to tell others what had happened. The smoke was a message, so others in faraway places could see it and understand what had happened. Then, people learned to write. Still some things needed to be kept secret. So they used numbers to mean letters or words. 1 means A, 2 means B, and 26 means Z.

1	2	3	4	5	6	7	8	9	10	11	12	13
A	B	C	D	E	F	G	H	I	J	K	L	M
14	15	16	17	18	19	20	21	22	23	24	25	26
N	O	P	Q	R	S	T	U	V	W	X	Y	Z

Jimmy has written a message for Amy. Someone might read it, so he writes his way: 13-5-5-20 13-5 1-20 19-3-8-15-15-12.

The message is, MEET ME AT SCHOOL.

Now, we have a message for you. Can you read it?

2-5 1 7-15-15-4 19-20-21-4-5-14-20

23. Which set of numbers spell "happy"?

  A. 8-1-18-18-9.

  B. 8-1-20-20-25.

  C. 8-1-16-16-25.

Join the Kids' New Year Party

Time: *7:00p.m., Dec.31*
Place: *Happy Children's Home*
(260 Da-lin Road)

There's a New Year party for the kids at Happy Children's Home. You are welcome to come and play with them.

P.S. Do you have books or toys for kids? If you don't need them anymore, you can give yours to the kids at Happy Children's Home. Please bring your books or toys to Ms. Love at Happy Children's Home from 9:00a.m. to 6:00p.m. before December 28.

24. What does the Happy Children's Home ask for?

    A. Toys.

    B. Books.

    C. Both of the above.

Read Tom's diary and answer the questions.

March 16, 2018

Today I met an American on my way home. He asked me some questions in English. I knew his words, but I was nervous and couldn't say anything. But my friend, David, talked to him happily. I felt so depressed. I study English very hard and get the best grades on English tests. But I just can't speak. However, David is not good at taking tests, but he listens to English radio programs and sometimes calls in to talk to the DJs in English. I think I have to practice speaking English more.

25. Why is Tom depressed?

    A. He's not as good at math as David.

    B. He's not as good at speaking English as David.

    C. He's not as good at taking tests as David.

26. Gina wants two hamburgers. How much will she pay?

    A. $60.

    B. $80.

    C. $120.

The Recipe of Granny's Sugar Cookies

The things you need

- 1c. sugar
- 2c. flour
- 2 tsp. baking soda
- 2 eggs
- 1/2 c. milk

First, mix the sugar, flour, and baking soda in a bowl. In another bowl, mix the eggs and milk. Then, mix the two bowls together slowly. Shape the dough into star shapes. Bake at 180°C for 25 minutes.

27. How much salt does Granny's Sugar Cookie recipe call for?

   A. 1 cup.

   B. 2 teaspoons.

   C. None.

Hi, I'm Jim. Look! This is my bedroom. It's not very big, but it's very clean. My desk is near the window. The light there is very good. On the desk is a notebook. I can surf the Net with it. Sometimes I play computer games on it, too. My bed is next to the door. My pet cat, Meow-Meow, likes to sleep on it. There is no TV in my room, and there is no telephone in it, either. My parents want me to study hard and be a doctor one day.

28. Which picture is Jim's bedroom?

A.
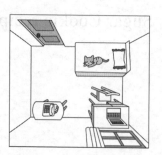

B.
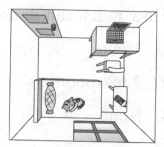

C.
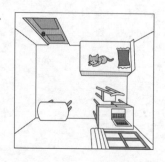

Big Dog Happy Bus Vacation

NT$ 4,000 each

Every Tuesday to Friday

※ See the koalas at Taipei City Zoo.

※ Shop in the biggest shopping mall — great!

※ Enjoy two nights at the 5-star Royal Hotel.

Day 1: Leave Kaohsiung at 8 a.m.

        – Have lunch in Tainan

        – Buy delicious sun cakes in Taichung

        – Get to Taipei at 9 p.m.

Day 2: Visit Taipei Zoo and Yangmingshan National Park.

Day 3: Go shopping all over the city.

29. What will you see at Taipei City Zoo?
    A. Koalas.
    B. Sun cakes.
    C. The biggest shopping mal.

Dear Allen,

There is a great basketball game at the gym this afternoon. In my pocket, there are three tickets to the game. Sam is going to the game with me. How about you? Are you also a basketball fan? Come with us! Let's go together and cheer for those great players. Call me at 0931-827-394.

Tom

Dear Tom,

Yes. I am a very big basketball fan. But I'm going to Amy's house this afternoon. Today is her birthday, and we are going to a movie. I'm in the library now. There is no pay phone here, so I can't call you. Call Amy and ask her to go to the ball game. Maybe you, Sam, Amy, and I can go together.

Allen

30. What does Allen suggest?

A. Selling the tickets.

B. Going to the game as a group.

C. Watching the game on TV.

TEST 2

閱讀：是非題

請仔細閱讀，看看句子和圖片的內容是不是一樣呢？如果相同，請在答案
卡上塗黑 Y；如果不同，請塗黑 N。

1. The girl is washing her hair.
2. The man is watching TV.

正確答案： 1. N　　2. N

1. Mr. Smith is wearing shorts.
2. Mr. Smith is now 66 years old.

3. The old woman is sitting on the bench.

4. The young girl is sitting on the bench.

5. Judy would like a new bicycle for Christmas.

6. Judy is wearing a hat.

7. The boy has a ball.

8. The boy has a stuffed animal.

9. The man is studying Chinese.

10. The woman has curly hair.

11. The boy is watching television.

12. The man is in front of the boy.

13. They are riding a bus.

14. They are seated on a couch.

15. Mr. Chang is a doctor.

16. Mrs. Chang is a teacher.

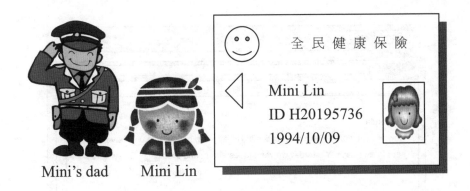

17. Mini's father is a singer.

18. Mini was born in 1994.

19. Tina is working on a math problem.

20. Tina is wearing glasses.

閱讀：選擇題

作答說明：閱讀後，每題請根據文章內容選出一個最適合的答案，在答案卡上作答。

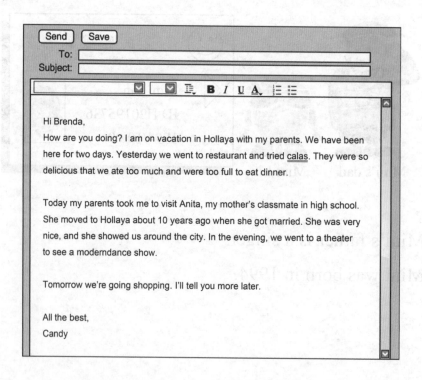

Hi Brenda,

How are you doing? I am on vacation in Hollaya with my parents. We have been here for two days. Yesterday we went to restaurant and tried calas. They were so delicious that we ate too much and were too full to eat dinner.

Today my parents took me to visit Anita, my mother's classmate in high school. She moved to Hollaya about 10 years ago when she got married. She was very nice, and she showed us around the city. In the evening, we went to a theater to see a moderndance show.

Tomorrow we're going shopping. I'll tell you more later.

All the best,
Candy

Where is Candy now?

A. At school.

B. At work.

C. On vacation.

正確答案：C

Have a nice trip!

Thailand	New Zealand (7 days)
A nice stay at Grand Hotel	*Farm visit
-3 days 2 nights	*Bungee jumping
-body massage	*Boat trip
-cooking class	September
-August 1-31	Only NT$50,000 (a person)
(every Sunday)	
-NT$20,000	
Cruise Europe	INDIA (6 days)
July 15-31, 7 days	-Temple visits
NT$200,000	-Elephant rides
For two people	Special low price:
	NT$32,000
	Date: August 20-26

21. Oscar wants to ride an elephant. Where should he go?

    A. New Zealand.

    B. Europe.

    C. India.

It's dark. Mark and Beth are at home. Their dad and mom are still at school. Mark is very hungry, and Beth is, too. They want to eat something. Look! Two big cakes are on the kitchen table. One is for Mark, and the other is for Beth. The cakes are so yummy. Mark hopes he can eat one every day.

---

22. What is true about Mark and Beth?

    A. They are still at school.

    B. They are at home with their parents.

    C. They are very hungry.

I am Jimmy. I study in the Elementary School. Look at these photos. These are the people in my family. This is my grandpa. He lives on a farm. My dad and mom are cooks. They have a restaurant. This is my uncle. He's very cool. He's a firefighter. My sister works in a hospital, and my brother works in a factory. Look! He is holding a robot.

23. What is true about Jimmy's uncle?

    A. He lives on a farm.

    B. He owns a restaurant.

    C. He is a firefighter.

Brian comes from the U.S.A., but he's now living and studying in Tainan. Christmas is his favorite holiday, but he doesn't know much about Chinese New Year.

Today is February 2nd. Chinese New Year is two weeks away. Brian's good friend, George, will invite Brian to his house for the New Year. On Chinese New Year's Eve, George's family will have a big dinner. They'll have chicken, fish, dumplings, and many other delicious dishes. After dinner, they'll watch TV, make some tea and talk more about the customs for Chinese New Year. George's parents will also give Brian a red envelope with NT$3,600 inside. It will be Brian's first time to get "lucky money."

24. Where will Brian spend Chinese New Year?
    A. With his family in the U.S.
    B. With his classmates in Taichung.
    C. With George's family in Tainan.

After school, I like to go to the park with my friends. I like to play basketball with Peter, Mike and Kevin. Joe and Jack like to fly a kite. Tim likes to climb a tree. Jay likes to read under a tree. I usually have a good time with my friends in the park.

25. Who likes to read under a tree?

    A. Jay.

    B. Joe.

    C. Jack.

Shopping at Home

"What? It's Mother's Day? Oh, I have been so busy these days. I haven't bought a present for my mom!"

"Oh! I forgot today's Mary's birthday! What should I do? The stores are all closed!"

Do you ever have these problems? Don't worry. Now you have Last Moment. More than 3,000 presents are ready for you at www.lastmoment5.com. Buy one on the computer, and we will send it to you ON THE SAME DAY or THE NEXT DAY!

www.lastmoment5.com

26. What is Last Moment?

   A. An online shopping service.

   B. A computer repair shop.

   C. A party planning company.

Fun Weekly Magazine

Issue 100   June 10

27. Ivan wants to read about basketball. What page should he turn to?

    A. Page 12.

    B. Page 14.

    C. Page 26.

Here are the evening TV programs on four channels		
TV Channel	Time	Program
Channel 12	6:30	News and Weather
	7:00	NBA Show
	8:00	MTV Time
Channel 23	6:00	Movie: Mulan
	8:00	Movie: A Dog's Story
	9:30	Movie: Avatar
Channel 36	6:00	Martha's Kitchen
	7:00	Let's Go to Hong Kong
	8:00	Wild Animals
Channel 60	6:30	News of the Week
	7:30	World News
	8:00	Taiwan News

28. Which channel(s) feature news programs?

A. Channel 36 only.

B. Channels 23 and 36.

C. Channels 12 and 60.

Grandma had a busy day yesterday. She got up at 6:30 in the morning and had breakfast with her grandchildren. After breakfast, Grandma took them to school. Then she taught piano lessons. She had some rice and chicken for lunch at 1:00 p.m. After lunch, she went to a supermarket for some vegetables and fruit.

But in the supermarket, she saw a thief stealing things. She caught him and called the police. Then, Grandma went home and cooked dinner.

29. What DIDN'T Grandma do yesterday?
    A. Catch a thief.
    B. Teach piano.
    C. See a movie.

Noise can hurt our hearing. Usually, we hear the best when we are 12 or 13 years old. As we get older, we don't hear as well. How much of our hearing do we lose? It is up to the noise around us. For example, people will lose some of their hearing if they work for a long time in noisy factories or in night clubs. Subways and motorcycles are other big noise-makers. However, a supersonic plane makes louder noise than any other noise-maker. We really live in a world full of noise.

30. Who is most likely to have hearing loss?

A. People who work in a library.

B. People who work in factories.

C. People who live on a farm.

TEST 3

閱讀：是非題

請仔細閱讀，看看句子和圖片的內容是不是一樣呢？如果相同，請在答案卡上塗黑 Y；如果不同，請塗黑 N。

1. The girl is washing her hair.
2. The man is watching TV.

正確答案：1. N   2. N

1. There is a telephone on the desk.
2. There is clock on the desk.

3. The boys are riding bicycles.

4. Each boy is carrying a ball.

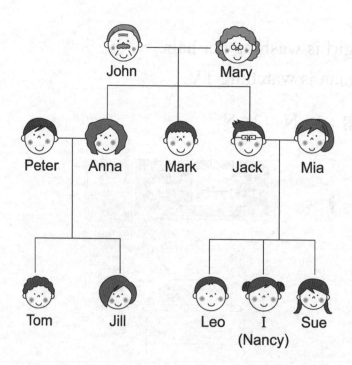

5. John and Mary have five children.

6. Mia is Sue's mother.

7. Kate is taking pictures of some buildings.

8. There are some boats in the harbor.

9. Jimmy loves his pets.

10. Jimmy is taking care of his fish.

There are 18 boys and 14 girls in Class 103. The following table shows us what activities they like to do after school:

Activities	Boy	Girl
Play basketball	12	9
Play video games	13	13
Chat with friends online	9	12
Watch TV	12	10
Listen to music	8	10
Ride bikes	4	4

11. Listening to music is the most popular activity among boys.

12. Both boys and girls like to play video games.

Airline	Flight	Time	Destination
China Airlines	CI012	08:00	New York
EVA Air	BR87	23:50	Paris
China Airlines	CI0222	08:45	Tokyo
EVA Air	BR67	09:10	London

13. The flight for New York leaves at 8:00.

14. EVA Air doesn't fly to London.

15. There are three trees.

16. The aquarium is in the middle.

	7/04	7/05	7/06	7/07	7/08
	Go to a movie	Clean the house	Play baseball	Piano class	Watch TV
Annie	O		O		O
Mary				O	O
Frank	O	O	O		O
Mike		O		O	O

17. Mike and Mary will see a movie.

18. Annie will clean the house.

19. These are pineapples.

20. The fruit costs 70 dollars.

閱讀：選擇題

作答說明：閱讀後，每題請根據文章內容選出一個最適合的答案，在答案卡上作答。

| Send | Save |

To:
Subject:

B *I* U A ≣ ≣

Hi Brenda,

How are you doing? I am on vacation in Hollaya with my parents. We have been here for two days. Yesterday we went to restaurant and tried <u>calas</u>. They were so delicious that we ate too much and were too full to eat dinner.

Today my parents took me to visit Anita, my mother's classmate in high school. She moved to Hollaya about 10 years ago when she got married. She was very nice, and she showed us around the city. In the evening, we went to a theater to see a moderndance show.

Tomorrow we're going shopping. I'll tell you more later.

All the best,
Candy

Where is Candy now?

A. At school.

B. At work.

C. On vacation.

正確答案：C

Hi, my name is Andy Wu. I have a brother and two sisters. They are Bill, Lisa, and Sally. Lisa is a student. She likes to play computer games, but we don't have a computer at home. This Christmas, Lisa wants a computer. Bill doesn't like computers. They're not easy for him. He wants a new basketball. He and his friends play basketball every weekend. My little sister, Sally, wants a bicycle. What about me? This year, I want a dog. After school, I can play with it. Everyone is happy on Christmas.

21. What does Sally want for Christmas?

    A. A new basketball.

    B. A dog.

    C. A bicycle.

Do you love panda bears? They're big, cute and shy. Two new visitors, Tuan-tuan and Yuan-yuan, just came from Szu-chuan last December. But remember not to get too close. There was an interesting story about a man and a panda.

This man had too much wine and went alone to Beijing Zoo. He climbed in and said hello to the pandas. He found one panda and tried to shake its hand. But instead, the panda took the man, turned him over and started to bite his leg! The man wasn't happy and tried to bite the panda on the back.

The panda's keeper saw what was happening and got the man out. Luckily, the man was not hurt. It is a good thing he tried to hug a panda, not a tiger!

22. Why did the man try to greet the panda?

A. He was drunk.

B. He was afraid.

C. He was from Szu-chuan.

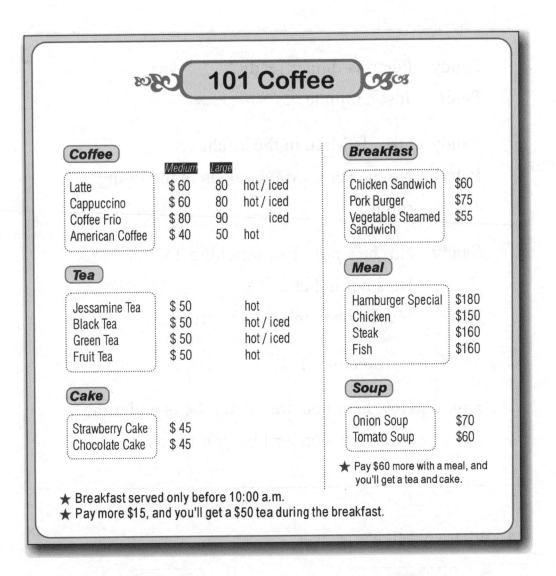

101 Coffee

Coffee

	Medium	Large	
Latte	$ 60	80	hot / iced
Cappuccino	$ 60	80	hot / iced
Coffee Frio	$ 80	90	iced
American Coffee	$ 40	50	hot

Tea

Jessamine Tea	$ 50	hot
Black Tea	$ 50	hot / iced
Green Tea	$ 50	hot / iced
Fruit Tea	$ 50	hot

Cake

Strawberry Cake	$ 45
Chocolate Cake	$ 45

Breakfast

Chicken Sandwich	$60
Pork Burger	$75
Vegetable Steamed Sandwich	$55

Meal

Hamburger Special	$180
Chicken	$150
Steak	$160
Fish	$160

Soup

Onion Soup	$70
Tomato Soup	$60

★ Pay $60 more with a meal, and you'll get a tea and cake.

★ Breakfast served only before 10:00 a.m.
★ Pay more $15, and you'll get a $50 tea during the breakfast.

23. Thomas had the steak meal and a cup of onion soup.

How much did he pay?

A. $210.

B. $220.

C. $230.

Sandy : Peter, is dinner ready?

Peter　: Just a minute.

Sandy : OK. Is Mike in the kitchen?

Peter　: No, he isn't. Maybe he is in the living room.

Sandy : No, he's not. I'm watching TV here. He's not in here.

Peter　: Maybe he is in Dad's bedroom.

　　(*Meow...meow...*)

Sandy : Hey, here you are. Peter, he is under the sofa. No wonder I couldn't see him.

24. Where is Mike?

A.

B.

C.

Today is January 18, 2018. Dr. Wang is still very busy. His chart falls on the floor. He needs to match the charts with the patients now. Please help him.

Name: **Chester**	Name: **Johnson**	Name: **Emily**
Age: 12	Age: 15	Age: 14
Cavities: 15	Cavities: 6	Cavities: 0
Last appointment: December 29, 2016	Last appointment: August 25, 2017	Last appointment: December 18, 2017

	I brush and floss my teeth after meals. I don't have any cavities. I visited the dentist every six months.
	I should brush my teeth more often. I care about having healthy teeth. I want to have beautiful teeth.
	I love to eat candy. I hate going to the dentist's office. My parents tell me to brush my teeth every day, but I don't.

25. Who takes the best care of his/her teeth?

   A. Chester.

   B. Johnson.

   C. Emily.

Mr. Farmer : Good morning, everyone. I'm Andy Farmer, your English teacher. Let's talk about your favorite sports star. Jeff, who is your favorite sports star?

Jeff : Well, my favorite sports star is a swimmer. His name is Michael Phelps.

Mr. Farmer : Is he from Canada?

Jeff : No, he and I are Americans.

Mr. Farmer : OK. How about you, Peter?

Peter : My favorite sports star is a basketball player. He is Michael Jordan.

26. Who is Peter's favorite sports star?

A.    B.

C.

A. Dear Graduates

Which teacher do you want to say "Thank you" to most? Do you want to share every interesting thing you had here?

B. Dear Schoolmates

Do you have any funny jokes to share? Have you taken any photos of our beautiful school?

C. Dear Teachers

Do you have any words to tell the graduates? Do you want to recommend to all of us any books to read carefully?

You are welcome to contribute your work! Please hand them in to Class 813, Clair Chen.

- **Note:**
  1. The deadline is November 30.
  2. If your work is chosen, you will get a present from us.

27. Who might have some words of advice?

    A. Graduates.

    B. Schoolmates.

    C. Teachers.

Everyone knows tea comes from China, but how did it become the favorite drink in England? Tea was probably the national drink of China and Japan in the 16th century. During this time, explorers from Europe found this interesting drink and brought it back to their countries. Holland was the first country to import tea from China. It then exported it to England.

Tea soon became very popular in England but not only as a drink. The English people believed that tea was good for health and that it was also a kind of medicine. By 1750, tea was the favorite beverage of all classes in this country.

28. What was the first country to import tea from China?
    A. Japan.
    B. Holland.
    C. England.

Dear Amanda,

I am a worried 13-year-old student. I am doing very well at school, but I am not happy with the way I look. My nose is big, and I wear glasses. I am quite fat, too! My friends tell me not to worry and remember to go jogging every day. My mom wants me to stop eating too much chocolate and candy. Other kids can eat as much as they like. Why can't I? The more I worry, the more I eat. What should I do?

Ugly Duckling in Swan High School

29. What is Ugly Duckling worried about?

    A. His appearance.

    B. His grades.

    C. His parents.

Throughout the world, different peoples get clean in different ways. For example, the English always take a bath. They sit in a bathtub full of warm water. But most Americans don't like it that way. They like taking showers. The Japanese first wash with soap in the shower. Then they go and sit in a bathtub of warm water. The Thais wash in a room and pour water from a jar on themselves. They wear a long piece of cloth, so that other people do not see their bodies.

The ways of cleaning their bodies may be different for people, but they all know that it is good to be clean, and that soap and water are good for health.

30. Who prefers taking showers?

A. American people.

B. English people.

C. Thai people.

TEST 4

閱讀：是非題

請仔細閱讀，看看句子和圖片的內容是不是一樣呢？如果相同，請在答案卡上塗黑 Y；如果不同，請塗黑 N。

1. The girl is washing her hair.
2. The man is watching TV.

正確答案：1. N   2. N

Mon.	Tues.	Wed.	Thurs.	Fri.	Sat.	Sun.

1. Monday's forecast calls for snow.
2. Friday's forecast calls for sunny skies.

Jenny

3. Jenny is eating a sandwich.

4. Jenny is very happy.

5. Paul is using a computer.

6. Linda is talking on the phone.

7. It is sunny in Hualien.

8. It is raining in Hsinchu.

9. The 12th is circled on the calendar.

10. There are 30 days in the month.

11. The farmer is planting his crops.

12. There are two main growing seasons.

13. The man drives to work.

14. It takes the man 30 minutes to drive to work.

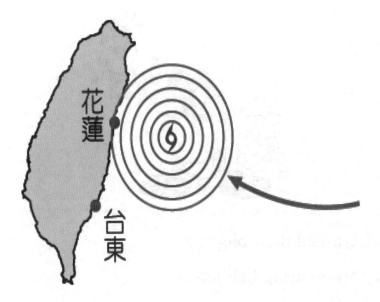

15. The typhoon is headed for the east coast of Taiwan.

16. The typhoon will be stronger in Hualien than Taitung.

17. The woman is upset.

18. The man is laughing.

19. They crashed their bicycles.

20. They are wearing helmets.

閱讀：選擇題

作答說明：閱讀後，每題請根據文章內容選出一個最適合的答案，在答案卡上作答。

Send　Save

To:

Subject:

▽　▽　E. **B** *I* U A ☰ ☰

Hi Brenda,

How are you doing? I am on vacation in Hollaya with my parents. We have been here for two days. Yesterday we went to restaurant and tried calas. They were so delicious that we ate too much and were too full to eat dinner.

Today my parents took me to visit Anita, my mother's classmate in high school. She moved to Hollaya about 10 years ago when she got married. She was very nice, and she showed us around the city. In the evening, we went to a theater to see a moderndance show.

Tomorrow we're going shopping. I'll tell you more later.

All the best,
Candy

Where is Candy now?

A. At school.

B. At work.

C. On vacation.

正確答案：C

David's Schedule		
Sunday	9:00 a.m.	have breakfast with Sue
Monday	11:00 a.m.	go shopping for food
Tuesday	2:00 p.m.	go swimming
Wednesday	4:00 p.m.	see a movie
Thursday	10:30 a.m.	meet Mr. Li
Friday	8:30 a.m.	play tennis with Jane
Saturday	5:30 a.m.	go hiking
	9:00 a.m.	have breakfast with Sue
	3:30 p.m.	teach Mary English

21. David is meeting with Mr. Li right now. What day is it?

    A. Tuesday.

    B. Wednesday.

    C. Thursday.

Sally : What are you doing?

Edward : My computer is out of order. I am looking for a new one.

Sally : What are you going to do with your old computer?

Edward : That's a problem. I have no idea.

Sally : You can sell it.

Edward : It's pretty old, and it can't be used.

Sally : Maybe some of its parts can be used. I know some computer stores take your computer and recycle it. And you can get some money too.

Edward : That's great! Tell me their phone numbers. I am going to call them tonight.

Sally : Sure. Before you call, make sure you move all the information from your old computer to your new one.

22. What does Sally suggest?

A. Recycling the computer.

B. Buying a new computer.

C. Fixing his computer.

Too many old books you won't read anymore?

Want to read different books
but also want to save money?

GREEN BOOK PEOPLE can help!

This is how we work:

◎ **List your books on our website for sale.**

For each book sold, you will receive $50.

◎ **Buy any book on our website for $60 each,**

and we put $10 to good use:

We plant trees.

Visit www. greenbookpeople.com.tw to start
your green reading life now!

23. What is NOT something Green Book People does?

A. Plant trees.

B. Sell books.

C. Buy books.

ABC Convenience Store ---

Collect Stickers to Win

1	2	3	4	5	6	7	8	9	10
11	12	13	14	15	16	17	18	19	20

- For every NT$30 you spend, you can get a sticker.

- Place the stickers in the grid.

- Collect 20 stickers, and you can get a toy car for only fifty dollars.

24. Ted just spent NT$330 at ABC Convenience Store. How many stickers did he receive?

A. 9.

B. 10.

C. 11.

 **RoboCup is a world soccer event. It began in 1997 and takes place in a different country each year. Many fans come to cheer for their favorite team. But there's something special --- all the players are robots. Scientists from different countries make teams of robots. They run, catch a ball, and pass a ball to each other. With the hard work of scientists, robots can play better and better. Scientists even want the robots to beat teams of people before 2050. Is it possible? Let's wait and see. Also, RoboCup has special games for teenagers. School students like you can make robots and join Junior Robo. Sounds interesting, right?**

25. What is true about RoboCup?

    A. The game is played by robots.

    B. The robots are better than people.

    C. Only scientists are allowed to participate.

My name is Ken. I'm from Taiwan. I am a junior high school student. I love books and all subjects at school. I read about two books every week. Einstein is my favorite scientist.

I'm Jean. I come from the UK. I am a violin tutor. I train many students and they become excellent violin players. We get together and play the violin every Wednesday. We really enjoy music and have fun.

I'm David. I'm from Canada. These are my pets, Choco and Milk. Choco is a small dog. She has a big nose and short ears. She likes to sleep. Milk is a big dog. He has short hair and a big mouth. He likes to catch a Frisbee. I love them.

26. What do Ken, Jean, and David have in common?

A. They all love music.

B. They all live in Taiwan.

C. Nothing.

Every student needs a place to study. Some students like to study in the quiet atmosphere of a library. Most school libraries have large study tables with many chairs. They also have individual study booths called carrels. Other students prefer to study in their own rooms at home or in a dormitory. And all students need comfortable chairs because they spend many hours on them.

Students have different ideas about the best atmosphere for studying. Some students listen to music or study in groups. Other students need to be alone in a quiet room. In others words, there is no best atmosphere for studying, there is a best atmosphere for each individual student.

27. What do all students need?

A. A comfortable chair.

B. A quiet atmosphere.

C. Other students.

5	3			7				
6			1	9	5			
	9	8					6	
8				6				3
4			8		3			1
7				2				6
	6					2	8	
			4	1	9			5
				8			7	9

Su Doku is a number puzzle. The aim of Su Doku is to enter a number from 1 to 9 in each box in a big table. The big table is made up of nine small tables. Each of them has nine boxes. A few numbers have already been given in each small table. Each number must only appear once in each row, column and small table.

No one knows who made the first Su Doku, but the game first appeared in print in New York in the late 1970s. In April 1984, a Japanese man, Maki Kaji, brought the game to his country. Later, people called the game Su Doku.

28. What is the reading about?

A. It is about why Su Doku has been so popular.

B. It is about how to fill in a Su Doku.

C. It is about the person who made the first Su Doku.

I had a dream—a strange dream, and it helped me to understand John much better.

I've lived with John for more than five years. He is the cutest thing in the world. I buy him fish and milk and lots of toy mice. I even bought a small house for him, because he sometimes likes to be alone. I love him with all my heart.

But what went wrong? In the dream, John looked angry and said to me, "Tracy, I have something to tell you. I don't like fish. I don't like milk. And toy mice? Are you crazy? I'm not a cat. And I don't want to be a cat, either!" Then he ran back to his small house.

After the dream, I know better: dogs don't like fish or milk. And surely they don't like toy mice. Besides, they will let you know when they are really angry!

29. Who or what is John?

   A. A fish.

   B. A cat.

   C. A dog.

There are 40 students in Daisy's class. The following pie chart shows what Daisy and her classmates do during weekdays.

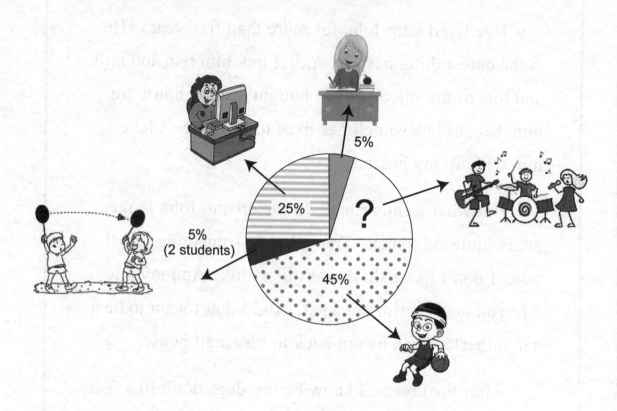

30. How many students play music during weekdays?

A. 8.

B. 10.

C. 12.

TEST 5

閱讀：是非題

請仔細閱讀，看看句子和圖片的內容是不是一樣呢？如果相同，請在答案卡上塗黑 Y；如果不同，請塗黑 N。

1. The girl is washing her hair.
2. The man is watching TV.

正確答案：1. N   2. N

1. They caught the fish they will soon eat.

2. They are seated at a table.

3. This is a birthday party.

4. There are three presents on the table.

5. They probably know each other.

6. It's a sunny day.

7. Josh likes to play soccer.

8. Josh is a good swimmer.

9. The museum was built in 1960.

10. The museum contains art.

11. Jack is Bill's father.

12. Tom and Doris are siblings.

13. The robots are scaring the boy.

14. The boy is pointing at the robots.

8/27 MOVIES

15. There are three movies scheduled for August 27.

16. The girl wants to see the animated film.

17. The moon is full.

18. They are having breakfast.

19. She is probably late for class.

20. There is a flag atop the school.

閱讀：選擇題

作答說明：閱讀後，每題請根據文章內容選出一個最適合的答案，在答案卡上作答。

Send　Save

To:
Subject:

▼　▼　Ⅰₑ　**B** *I* U A̱　⦙Ξ　⦙Ξ

Hi Brenda,

How are you doing? I am on vacation in Hollaya with my parents. We have been here for two days. Yesterday we went to restaurant and tried <u>calas</u>. They were so delicious that we ate too much and were too full to eat dinner.

Today my parents took me to visit Anita, my mother's classmate in high school. She moved to Hollaya about 10 years ago when she got married. She was very nice, and she showed us around the city. In the evening, we went to a theater to see a moderndance show.

Tomorrow we're going shopping. I'll tell you more later.

All the best,
Candy

Where is Candy now?

A. At school.

B. At work.

C. On vacation.

正確答案：C

On top of the green leaves she proudly stands.

Pretty girls love to hold her in their hands.

Red, pink, purple, and white.

She looks so graceful in the moonlight.

To pick her, you must be careful.

Because she's as dangerous as beautiful.

---

21. What does "she" look like?

A.    B.

C.

Two Letters

Dear Bill,

I am sorry, but it's time to say goodbye. I have a new boyfriend. Would you please send my photos back? I want to give them to my new boyfriend.

Susan

Dear Susan,

Sorry, I have too many girlfriends. Please find your photos by yourself.

Bill

22. What does Susan want from Bill?

A. Her photos.

B. Her love letters.

C. An apology.

(Linda is a new student in the Junior High School. She is talking with Sally.)

Linda : Nice to meet you. I am Linda.

Sally : Nice to meet you, too. My name is Sally.

Linda : Sally, what time is our English class today?

Sally : Today is Monday. Our English class is at eight and our Chinese class is at ten.

Linda : Thank you. Is the music class at one thirty?

Sally : No, we have music classes on Tuesday morning and Thursday afternoon.

Linda : Isn't our PE class at two o'clock this afternoon?

Sally : Yes, we can play basketball and soccer.

Linda : Great. Who can we play with?

Sally : Little Mark.

Linda : You mean Mark Wells?

Sally : Yes, we have two Marks in our class. One is short and thin; the other is tall and a little heavy.

Linda : Hah. That's funny.

23. Who is "Little Mark"?

A. 　　B. 　　C.

Willy is a little boy.

He's from Taiwan.

Kitty and Birdie are his new friends.

Birdie is small and cute, and she's a good singer.

Kitty likes to sleep.

Fish is his favorite and he eats that every day.

Where are Kitty and Birdie?

Kitty is under the chair.

Birdie is in her small cage now.

By the way, Kitty is a black cat, and Birdie is a
    yellow bird.

They are very happy.

24. Who likes eating fish?

A. Willy.

B. Birdie.

C. Kitty.

Moon Cakes

From August 25 to September 10

10% off for each purchase over NT$1000

Fruit Moon Cake	Green Bean Moon Cake	Red Bean Moon Cake
NT$260 / box	NT$320 / box	NT$350 / box
Chocolate Moon Cake	Gold Moon Cake	Ice Cream Moon Cake
NT$350 / box	NT$650 / box	NT$720 / box

25. Mr. Fong bought two boxes of Ice Cream Moon Cakes.
   How much did he pay?
   A. NT$1,440.
   B. NT$1,320.
   C. NT$1,296.

Rules for visiting
Purple Butterfly Valley

There are some rules for you here.

* Do not catch the butterflies.

* Do not make noise.

* Do not shake trees.

* Do not pick flowers.

* Do not litter.

* Do not run.

* Do not talk on your cellphone.

26. What can you do at Purple Butterfly Valley?

A. Make noise.

B. Catch the butterflies.

C. Watch the butterflies.

Big Sale at Happy World

Item	Before	Now	Item	Before	Now
PC	US$600	US$500	camera	US$300	US$250
fridge	US$800	US$600	cellphone	US$200	US$150
printer	US$100	US$70	TV	US$500	US$350

Date: July first ~ July seventh

Open Hours: 10:00 ~ 21:00 (Tue-Fri); 9:30 ~ 22:00 (weekend)

27. Henry bought a camera and a cellphone.

   How much did he pay?

   A. US$500.

   B. US$400.

   C. US$250.

There are many holidays in a year. Some holidays are always on a certain date every year, like Valentine's Day, Halloween, and Christmas. Valentine's Day is on February 14, Halloween is on October 31, and Christmas is on December 25. Other holidays don't fall on fixed dates every year. For example, Mother's Day is on the second Sunday of May, and Thanksgiving is on the fourth Thursday of November. It's interesting, isn't it?

28. Which holiday falls on a fixed date every year?

A. Mother's Day.

B. Thanksgiving.

C. Halloween.

Yellow Dress

By Janet Lee

Mary had a yellow dress
Bought at the department store.
It looked as beautiful as the moon,
And as bright as the sun.
Mary wore it all the time.
The yellow dress felt so right.
Every day from day to night
I saw her in the dress so bright.
"Buy me a yellow dress,"
I cried to Mom and Dad,
"As beautiful and bright
As the dress the girl living near has!"
I cried and cried and cried,
Until they said with sad eyes,
"We need food for your baby sister,
And clothes for your coming brother."
Since then I've learned
Mary's yellow dress
Is better to dream of
Than to ask for.

29. What do we know about Janet's parents?

A. They are expecting a third child.

B. They both work full-time.

C. They don't like spoiling their children.

Find a Lost Dog

My dog, Lucy, was lost near school.

She is three years old.

Her brown hair is short.

Her cute nose is black.

She has big ears, short legs and a long tail.

If you find her, please contact Miss Lin.

Phone: 02-2244-7799

Cellphone: 0911-775-663

E-mail: lucydog@find.com

Reward for finding the dog: NT$3,000

Thank you for your help!

30. What do we know about Lucy?

A. She was lost near school.

B. She has long ears and a short tail.

C. Her owner is Mr. Lin.

TEST 6

閱讀：是非題

請仔細閱讀，看看句子和圖片的內容是不是一樣呢？如果相同，請在答案卡上塗黑 Y；如果不同，請塗黑 N。

1. The girl is washing her hair.
2. The man is watching TV.

正確答案：1. N　2. N

1. This is a farm.
2. The cows are resting.

3. Kevin is sitting across from Emma.

4. Bill is sitting behind Harry.

5. Ms. Davis is having a cup of tea.

6. Ms. Davis will water some flowers later.

7. Mr. Huang is in bed.

8. Mrs. Huang is a doctor.

9. August 7 is a special day.

10. There are 31 days in August.

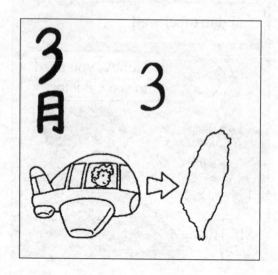

11. Jim will fly to Taiwan in March.

12. Jim will fly to the U.S. in April.

13. Jack is playing chess.

14. The fish is jumping out of the water.

15. Sarah likes playing the piano.

16. She usually practices in the morning.

	Tue.	Wed.	Thur.	Today
Keelung	rainy	rainy	rainy	rainy
New York	snowy	cloudy	rainy	snowy
London	cloudy	cloudy	rainy	cloudy
Kaohsiung	cloudy	sunny	rainy	sunny

17. It's cold in New York today.

18. It's sunny in Kaohsiung today.

Sun	Mon	Tue	Wed	Thu	Fri	Sat
	⚫		⚫			

19. Dave plays basketball on Monday and Wednesday.

20. Dave doesn't play basketball on Sunday.

閱讀：選擇題

作答說明：閱讀後，每題請根據文章內容選出一個最適合的答案，在答案卡上作答。

Send **Save**
To:
Subject:

☑ ☑ ☰ **B** *I* <u>U</u> **A** ☰ ☰

Hi Brenda,

How are you doing? I am on vacation in Hollaya with my parents. We have been here for two days. Yesterday we went to restaurant and tried calas. They were so delicious that we ate too much and were too full to eat dinner.

Today my parents took me to visit Anita, my mother's classmate in high school. She moved to Hollaya about 10 years ago when she got married. She was very nice, and she showed us around the city. In the evening, we went to a theater to see a moderndance show.

Tomorrow we're going shopping. I'll tell you more later.

All the best,
Candy

Where is Candy now?

A. At school.

B. At work.

C. On vacation.

正確答案：C

I'm Eliot, a twenty-year-old student. Leo is my classmate and roommate. We study English, play basketball, and swim at school during the day. We like our school life very much. After school, we study, write and read short stories. On Sunday, we fly a kite at the park. I'm a great writer, and Leo is a good singer. We help the kids in Opal Inn, too. They don't have parents and need our help. The kids Ming-Ming and Ding-Ding, call Leo "Big Hero." I like it! What do they call me? They call me "Handsome Egg"! "Handsome Egg" is my new short story. Ha!

21. What is Leo's nickname?

    A. Big Hero.

    B. Handsome Egg.

    C. Opal Inn Kid.

Amy buys some food at Denny's Shop. Here is her receipt.

Denny's Shop		2015-4-19 13:30 No.356416
Apples	5	NT$100
Eggs	10	NT$89
Fish	1	NT$119
Chicken	1	NT$85
Coffee	3	NT$75
Milk	1	NT$70
Orange juice	1	NT$70
Rice	1	NT$125
Bananas	5	NT$60
Total		NT$793

22. How much do bananas cost?

    A. NT$10 each.

    B. NT$12 each.

    C. NT$15 each.

To: pattylin@yahoo.com.tw
From: davidlin@yahoo.com.tw
Subject: The Gift for Mom
Date: Wednesday, August 10

Dear Patty,

    I called you many times, but you haven't called me back. Next Monday is Mom's birthday, and Dad will cook a big dinner for her on Sunday evening. So be sure to come home for dinner on Sunday. I plan to buy a smart phone for Mom. She often goes traveling with her friends. She can take many great pictures and send them to us with the smart phone. I think it's a cool gift for her. I checked the price of the smart phone, and it's NT$10,000. I think you can share the money with me. I pay half of it, and you pay the other half. What do you think about it? Please call me back as soon as possible. See you on Sunday!

Love,
David

23. What does David ask Patty?

    A. To share the cost of a gift.

    B. To help prepare a meal.

    C. To buy a new smart phone.

The following is Andy's weekend schedule.

Saturday	Sunday
7:00～12:00 take a train from Kaohsiung to Taipei	9:00～12:00 take a bus to Yangmingshan to watch birds
12:00～14:00 go to Hank's steak house by taxi and have lunch with my friends, Bella and Adam	12:00～14:00 have a picnic in the mountains
18:00～21:00 take the MRT to Shilin Night Market	14:00～15:00 go to Taipei Station by bus
21:00 walk to Adam's home	15:30 go back home by Taiwan High Speed Rail

24. Where will Andy spend Saturday night?

    A. In Kaohsiung.

    B. At Adam's house.

    C. In a hotel in Shilin.

Boy : Hi, Jean. Where are you going?

Girl : Hello, Jack. Nora and I are going to the park.

Boy : Why?

Girl : My brother, Kenny, has a big basketball game against Happy High School.

Boy : I see.

Girl : Why not go with me? I know basketball is your favorite sport.

Boy : I want to, but I can't. I have to stay at home with my brother, Sam. My parents aren't at home this afternoon.

Girl : You can take him there.

Boy : No, he's just three. He doesn't understand anything about basketball.

Girl : I see. I have to go now. The game begins at a quarter past three.

Boy : OK. See you.

Girl : Goodbye.

25. Why won't Jean take Sam to the park?

    A. He's too young.

    B. He's not feeling well.

    C. He's with his parents.

There's an English speech contest at Lisa's school this Friday. Many people in Lisa's class like English. They all study hard and speak well. Lisa wants to speak better, so she practices a lot. Lisa's teacher asked her to join the speech contest because Lisa speaks the best.

Lisa is excited about the contest, but she is also very nervous. She is afraid of making a mistake. Many people gave Lisa advice.

"Go to school early, so you can prepare," Lisa's mother said.

"Speak clearly, so everyone can hear easily," said Lisa's teacher.

However, the best advice was from Lisa's brother.

"Don't worry about making mistakes. Everyone makes mistakes sometimes," he said. "Try hard and do your best."

26. Who asked Lisa to join the speech contest?

A. Her mother.

B. Her brother.

C. Her teacher.

Hi, I'm Lisa! I come from America, and I'm thirteen years old. I love baseball. I play baseball with my brother, Ted, for two hours from Tuesday to Friday. Every day after school, I talk on the phone with Joan. Joan is my good friend. She is from Taiwan. She has long black hair and big eyes. She is a pretty girl! I especially love her small nose. It's cute! I play with Joan on weekends, too. On Saturday mornings, we have breakfast together, and then we go to the park. We jump rope there. On Sundays, we go to McDonald's for lunch, and then she goes home. After lunch, I go to the gym and exercise there. My cousin, Amy, is there, too. She is a good swimmer, and I am, too!

27. What does Lisa love most about her friend Joan?

    A. Her rope jumping skills.

    B. Her small nose.

    C. Her big eyes.

Give him a home

My dog Lulu has six baby puppies.

They're one month old.

They're weak and cute.

They're smart.

They will be your best friends.

They only need:

A little food, your love, and a warm house.

Now it's time to own them without paying anything.

If you want one, call me at 0900-123-456

I am happy to get your phone call.

Catherine

28. What should you do if you want a puppy?

A. Visit the animal shelter.

B. Call Catherine.

C. Buy one from the pet store.

Yummy Pizza

Small pizza: $300   **Large pizza: $500**

You can buy one large pizza, and get a small pizza free if you come to get the pizza yourself!

Cola $45   **Fried chicken** $70

Orange juice $60   **Apple pie** $50

Green tea $20

Telephone: 3938-3736

Open hours: Tuesday~ Sunday: 10:00 a.m.~ 9:00 p.m.

29. Which of the following is not a pizza topping?
    A. Chicken.
    B. Fish.
    C. Orange juice.

menu

Coffee..$150

Orange tea...$120

Milk tea...$100

Black tea..$90

Orange juice...$160

Apple juice..$160

Apple pie, banana cake, strawberry cake, chicken sandwich,

fish sandwich..$80

Afternoon tea set (Choose one drink and have all the desserts)

....$275

30. What is not included in the afternoon tea set for $275?

    A. Apple pie.

    B. Banana cake.

    C. Chicken sandwich.

TEST 7

閱讀：是非題

請仔細閱讀，看看句子和圖片的內容是不是一樣呢？如果相同，請在答案卡上塗黑 Y；如果不同，請塗黑 N。

1. The girl is washing her hair.
2. The man is watching TV.

正確答案：1. N　2. N

1. Charlotte plays the guitar.
2. She practices for half an hour every day.

3. This is a math class.

4. The students are learning English.

5. Ivy gets up the earliest.

6. Jill gets up the latest.

7. The buildings stand side by side.

8. The middle building is a KTV.

	Sat.	**Sun.**	**Mon.**
Jack		⚾	
Mary	⚾		🏸
Gary	🏸	🏸	⚾

9. Gary plays badminton more often than Jack.

10. Jack plays more baseball than Gary.

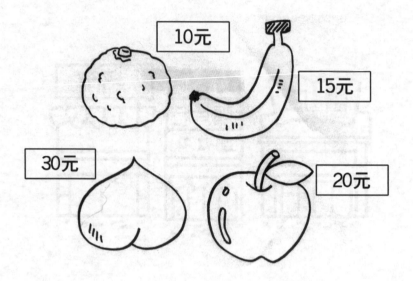

11. An apple costs 30 dollars.

12. A banana costs 15 dollars.

13. There are 10 men in the elevator.

14. The elevator is going down.

15. Gina weighs less than Lucy.

16. Lucy weighs 10 percent less than Gina.

17. Joanne has two dogs.

18. It's 6:00.

19. They are watching TV.

20. Bob is reading Harry Potter.

閱讀：選擇題

作答說明：閱讀後，每題請根據文章內容選出一個最適合的答案，在答案卡上作答。

Send Save

To:

Subject:

B I U A

Hi Brenda,

How are you doing? I am on vacation in Hollaya with my parents. We have been here for two days. Yesterday we went to restaurant and tried calas. They were so delicious that we ate too much and were too full to eat dinner.

Today my parents took me to visit Anita, my mother's classmate in high school. She moved to Hollaya about 10 years ago when she got married. She was very nice, and she showed us around the city. In the evening, we went to a theater to see a moderndance show.

Tomorrow we're going shopping. I'll tell you more later.

All the best,
Candy

Where is Candy now?

A. At school.

B. At work.

C. On vacation.

正確答案：C

Everyone has a favorite season. Fall is my mother's favorite one. She loves to go to Alishan and see the trees at the beginning of fall. The leaves all turn orange, red, and yellow. It is so beautiful. Every year, my whole family go there. My sister and I like to go there because we can run and play outside. We really enjoy the fresh air. My dad also likes to go there because the whole family can be together. We usually go there in Dad's car. It takes about four hours to get there from our house. On the way, we listen to music, tell stories, and talk. Sometimes, we are tired, and my mom, my sister and I sleep in the car. But my dad can't sleep. He is the driver!

---

21. How often does the family go to Alishan?

    A. Once a year.

    B. Twice a year.

    C. Every other month.

Granny's Kitchen Menu

Open Hours:　*Tuesday ~ Friday*　　*11:00 a.m. ~ 10:00 p.m.*

　　　　　　　　Saturday ~ Sunday　　*12:00 p.m. ~ 12:00 a.m.*

Salad

Chicken Salad　　NT$130

Caesar Salad　　NT$70

Fruit Salad　　NT$120

Main Dish

Double King Shrimp　　NT$320

Fried White Fish　　NT$300

Fried Chicken　　NT$310

Roasted Steak　　NT$290

Dessert

Strawberry Cake　NT$55

Apple Pie　　NT$45

Pudding　　NT$50

Drinks

Coffee/Tea (Hot/Iced)　NT$50

Orange Juice　　NT$60

Cola　　NT$50

Soup

Tomato Soup　　NT$80　　　　Soup of Day　　NT$50

(The prices above do not include 10% service charge)

◎ **Value Lunch** (only on Tuesday and Friday)

Set A

Salad 3 choose 1, Fried Chicken or Fish, only **NT$430**

Set B

Salad 3 choose 1, Double King Shrimp or Roasted Steak, only **NT$450**

* All value lunch sets include a main dish, a cup of soup, and a drink.
* You need to pay 10% service charge.

22. What is the service charge for Set B?

    A. NT$35.

    B. NT$43.

    C. NT$45.

Dear Terry:

    I saw your grades, and I'm not happy. Your father and I want to have a talk after he comes home. When you get home from school, take out the trash. Then water the flowers and do your homework. Don't forget to tell Ben not to come tonight. You need to do your homework. No video games or computer games. Your father and I will do something about your grades.

        See you tonight,

        Mom

23. What will Terry do tonight?

    A. Play video games.

    B. Do homework with Ben.

    C. Talk to his parents.

Dear Justin,   March 28

  My name is Kelly Anderson, and I am a thirteen-year-old girl from Boston, America. My favorite singer is Avril Lavigne. I love to listen to her songs before I go to bed.

  In my free time, I like to play with my smart dog, Lily. She can catch a Frisbee. We will join an animal contest this weekend. May God bless us.

  What do you like to do after school? I can't wait to hear from you soon.

Kelly

Justin Huang

NO. 123, Linyuan S. Rd.,

Linyuan District,

Kaohsiung City, 832,

Taiwan (R.O.C.)

24. Who is Justin Huang?

  A. Kelly's favorite singer.

  B. Kelly's classmate.

  C. Kelly's pen pal.

I had an accident and hurt my leg, and I couldn't go to school for a week. How did it happen? Well, I was riding very fast when a stupid cat suddenly came out to the street. The cat was fine, I didn't hit it, but I fell off my bike and my leg was hurt badly. So all I could do was lie in bed and rest. I turned on the TV in the afternoon, but my mom told me to turn it off. She said I needed to sleep and rest, and she took the remote control away from me. But having nothing to do really made me bored, so I started to read some English novels and I found they are quite interesting.

I went back to school today. I usually walk to school by myself, but it was raining today, so my mom drove me there. Both my classmates and the teachers are glad that I could come back to school to study. I was happy, too.

25. What happened to the cat?

   A. Its leg was badly hurt.

   B. It ran away from home and got lost.

   C. Nothing.

Look at the notice and answer the questions.

Pet Dog	Cindy's dog	Tom's dog	Andy's dog	Mary's dog
price	NT$15,000	NT$30,000	NT$45,000	NT$20,000
color	white	yellow	black	brown
size	small	medium	large	medium
weight	5 kg	10 kg	15 kg	10 kg
age	2 years old	8 months old	1 year old	20 months old

26. Who has the smallest dog?

A. Cindy.

B. Tom.

C. Mary.

Learning on Your Own

Food is important. Everyone needs to eat well if he or she wants to have a strong body. Our minds also need a kind of food. It's knowledge. We start getting knowledge when we are very young. Young children like watching and listening. They also like looking at color pictures. When children are older, they enjoy reading. They like learning about all kinds of things. They also love asking questions because they enjoy thinking about things and getting knowledge on their own. Our minds, like our bodies, always need the best food. When we get knowledge on our own, we enjoy learning. We also learn more and understand better.

27. Why do kids love asking questions?

   A. They are hungry for knowledge.

   B. They like to annoy adults.

   C. They think it will get them a better test score.

Lily's Bookstore	*Anniversary Sale!*	Dec. 1 ~ Dec. 31
Items	**Usual Price**	**Anniversary Sale**
Comic books	NT$300 each	20% off
Storybooks	NT$200 each	30% off
Magazines	NT$150 each	20% off
Dictionaries	NT$500 each	40% off
Albums	NT$400 each	20% off
CDs	NT$300 each	30% off
Open: Tue. ~ Sun.　10:30 a.m. ~ 10:00 p.m.		

28. Why is Lily's Bookstore having a sale?

　　A. To help the poor people.

　　B. To celebrate an anniversary.

　　C. To reward customer loyalty.

World Record Holder Asha Mandela has the longest hair. It is longer than a bus. Doctors warn that her hair, which weighs 66 pounds, could paralyze her. However, Asha Mandela said she will never cut it. She has grown her hair for twenty-five years. "My hair has become a part of me. It is my life. I will never cut it," said she. It takes two days to wash and dry her hair, which weighs the same as a child and is even heavier when wet. It can also get easily trapped in doors or on bushes. She has to fold it round into a baby sling when she leaves the house.

29. How long does it take to wash and dry Asha Mandela's hair?

    A. Two days.

    B. 66 pounds.

    C. Twenty-five years.

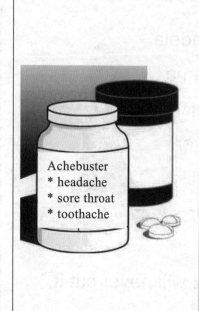

Achebuster
* headache
* sore throat
* toothache

< Directions >

* 12 years old and over: 2 tablets every four hours, three times a day

* 6 to 11 years old: 1 tablet every six hours, three times a day

* Children under 6 years old: consult a doctor

* Take with warm water after meals

* Keep in a cool, dry place

30. What is Achebuster good for?

A. Headaches.

B. Upset stomach.

C. Leg cramps.

TEST 8

閱讀：是非題

請仔細閱讀，看看句子和圖片的內容是不是一樣呢？如果相同，請在答案
卡上塗黑 Y；如果不同，請塗黑 N。

1. The girl is washing her hair.
2. The man is watching TV.

正確答案：1. N　2. N

1. They are building a snowman.
2. There are three boys and one snowman.

BOARDING PASS			
Name of Passenger: Sam Chen		From Taipei To New York	
FLIGHT	CLASS	DATE	TIME
TK1025	Y	May 19	13:10
GATE	BOARDING TIME	SEAT	SMOKE
16	12:30	35B	NO

3. Sam Chen will board the plane at 13:10.

4. The flight leaves from Gate 116.

5. Tina and Joe are sitting on the bench.

6. Leo is playing with the rabbits.

What Do They Do on Weekends?

	swim	play tennis	play dodge ball	roller-skate	go to English class
Nora	O	O		O	O
Edward		O			
Sunny	O			O	O
Paul	O		O		O

7. Nora is the most active on weekends.

8. Edward is the least active on weekends.

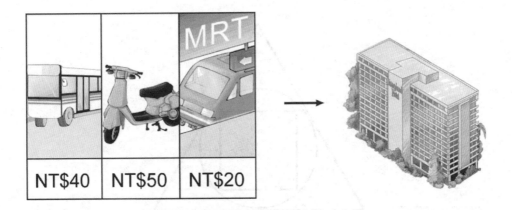

9. The MRT is the cheapest form of transportation to the hotel.

10. A bus to the hotel costs NT$40 dollars.

	Taipei	Taichung	Hualien	Kaohsiung
Friday	24℃	25℃	21℃	27℃
Saturday	22℃	20℃	26℃	29℃
Sunday	17℃	28℃	28℃	30℃

11. It's always hottest in Kaohsiung.

12. It's always coolest in Taipei.

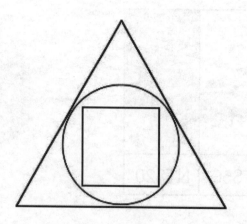

13. The square is inside the circle.

14. The circle is inside the triangle.

15. Bill will study for two hours.

16. Bill never studies in the library.

17. Food and drinks are not allowed.

18. Cameras are not allowed.

19. Dan will watch TV on Monday.

20. Dan will get some exercise on Friday.

閱讀：選擇題

作答說明：閱讀後，每題請根據文章內容選出一個最適合的答案，在答案卡上作答。

Send Save
To:
Subject:

B *I* U A ≣ ≡

Hi Brenda,

How are you doing? I am on vacation in Hollaya with my parents. We have been here for two days. Yesterday we went to restaurant and tried calas. They were so delicious that we ate too much and were too full to eat dinner.

Today my parents took me to visit Anita, my mother's classmate in high school. She moved to Hollaya about 10 years ago when she got married. She was very nice, and she showed us around the city. In the evening, we went to a theater to see a moderndance show.

Tomorrow we're going shopping. I'll tell you more later.

All the best,
Candy

Where is Candy now?

A. At school.

B. At work.

C. On vacation.

正確答案：C

This is a museum. There are rules for students to follow.

<u>DOs</u>

Wait in line.

Notice the signs on the wall.

Turn off your cellphone in the film room.

Have fun.

<u>DON'Ts</u>

Don't eat.

Don't take pictures.

Don't touch anything.

Don't talk in a loud voice.

---

21. What is it OK to do in the museum?

A. Have fun.

B. Eat.

C. Take pictures.

Mrs. Walker has one son. His name is Harry. When he was four years old, he had a child's bike. It was red and white. Then Harry had no bike for a long time. Now he's twelve years old, and he wants a bicycle. Mrs. Walker goes to work by car every day, and she takes Harry with her to his school, and brings him back after school. His school is on one side of the town, and Mrs. Walker's office is on the other side.

One day, Harry said to his mom, "A lot of my friends have bicycles, and they ride to school on them. Their mothers don't need to take them to school and bring them home again." But his mom said, "Wait, Harry. Your father and I are going to buy you a nice bike soon."

Then yesterday Mrs. Walker stopped her car at a red light and looked at Harry. "Harry, before I buy you a bike, I want to ask you something. Now, look at those traffic lights. Do you know their meaning?" "Oh, yes, I do!" Harry said happily. "Red is 'Stop', green is 'Go', and yellow is 'Go very quickly.'"

22. Does Harry know the meaning of the traffic lights?

A. Yes, he does.

B. No, he doesn't.

C. He only knows red and green.

Welcome to Happy Junior High School!

Here are some rules for you to enjoy sports in our school!

1. The playground is open from 5:30 p.m. to 8:00 p.m. from Monday to Friday and 3:00 p.m. to 7:00 p.m. on weekends.
2. No food or drinks on the playground.
3. It's for jogging, walking, and dancing only.
4. For baseball, please send your application one week before.
5. No pets on the playground.
6. Basketball is possible, too.

23. What time does the playground close on the weekend?

    A. 7:00 p.m.

    B. 8:00 p.m.

    C. 9:00 p.m.

Trees are the oldest living things on the Earth. Trees can live for more than 3,000 years. In fact, in the early twentieth century, big old trees were everywhere in Taiwan. At Alishan, more than 300,000 trees lived well. Some were taller than 12 meters and thicker than 10 meters.

Because they were so big and old, people showed respect to them by calling them "God Trees". Some of them were already there about 2,000 years ago.

Sadly, people began to cut them down for wood soon after they found these big trees. In a few decades, most of them were gone. These days, we have finally learned to protect the last few big trees. We hope our children and grandchildren can still see them standing tall.

24. What happened to the big old trees?

A. They were cut for wood.

B. They were sick.

C. They were burned in a fire.

This is a big kitchen. I smell something good.
Oh, there is some coffee and there are also some cakes
on the table. Under the table, there is a dog sleeping.
Next to it, there's a cat drinking milk. Mom is coming
into the kitchen. And then she will sit at the table and
drink the cup of coffee on the table.

25. Which picture is right?

A.

B.

C.

It's morning now. Jerry Green is at the park. He is playing basketball with his friend, Roy Jobs. Jerry's sister, May, and her grandpa are singing and laughing.

It's afternoon. Jerry and his family are on Uncle Ben's farm. There are many pretty farm animals. May is drawing rabbits. They are her favorite. And Jerry is riding a horse. Their parents are talking under a big tree, and their grandparents are feeding the monkeys near the tree.

It's evening now. The Green family is at home. They are having a party. They are very happy.

26. Who owns a farm?

A. Uncle Ben.

B. Grandpa.

C. Roy Jobs.

You ask what kind of person I am.

I speak out what I think,
Loud like an angry queen;
I stay low,
Quiet like a winter tree.

I'm excited,
As happy as a jumping rabbit;
I'm bored,
Feeling like a dead fish.

What kind of person am I?
Who knows?
I live and wear different faces,
Like everyone else.

27. What is true about the author?

A. Her moods are changeable.

B. She usually feels bored.

C. She is always happy.

Jay is going to Fisherman's Wharf from his house. There are three ways for him to get there.

Option 1		
Bus to Taipei Main Station	$20	30 mins
→ **MRT** from Taipei Station to Danshui	$55	40 mins
→ **Bus** to Fisherman's Wharf	$15	20 mins
Option 2		
Taxi to Xinpu MRT Station	$100	10 mins
→ **MRT** from Xinpu to Danshui	$65	60 mins
→ **Boat** to Fisherman's Wharf	$120	10 mins
Option 3		
Bus to Danshui	$50	110 mins
→ **Walk** to Fisherman's Wharf	$0	45 mins

28. Which option is the fastest?

    A. Option 1.

    B. Option 2.

    C. Option 3.

Mr. and Mrs. Wu are busy, so their three children help them to do the housework. Sheila is eighteen years old, and she has to take care of Sally and Sandy. She likes to tell stories to her sisters. Sally mops the floor and waters the plants at nine fifteen. Sandy walks the dog in the park at four ten. They also practice singing songs at five o'clock and make dinner together for their parents. Though the three girls are tired and busy, they still say "I love you." to their parents. It's really a sweet family.

29. Who mops the floor?

   A. Sheila.

   B. Sally.

   C. Sandy.

May's Clinic	
Name: Lee, Huei-hua	Date: 2018/7/2
ID No.: A123456789	For: _3_ days

Directions ☑ Take one dose before each meal

☐ Take one dose after each meal

☑ Take one dose before going to bed

☐ Morning ☐ Noon ☐ Evening

(Take one more dose)

☑ Take one dose when having a fever

☑ Take the medicine with warm water

Time: Monday～Saturday

Address: 170, Fu-sin 2nd Rd, Kaohsiung

(close on Sundays and holidays)

Telephone: (07) 6412059

● 09:00 A.M.～12:00 P.M.

● 03:00 P.M.～05:00 P.M.

● 07:00 P.M.～09:00 P.M

30. How should the medicine be taken?

A. With warm water.

B. On an empty stomach.

C. Using only clean needles.